Sharp lemon sponge filled with a creamy lemon buttercream and sweet raspberry conserve

Over the next few pages you will learn how to bake and fill a 6" round lemon & raspberry sponge.

The finished cake will be approx 5" tall, made up of 4 layers of cake and 3 layers of filling.

You will bake 2 x 6" round cakes, each approx 2.5" tall, and you will learn how cut and assemble the cake.

This is more than just a recipe. This is a full guide to baking and filling a cake, including troubleshooting tips and tricks.

Each step has full detailed instructions along with photos to ensure success every time.

The Sponge Ingredients ⟹

Lemon Sponge

For the sponge you will need:

- 2 x 6" round tins (3" deep)
- Greaseproof, nonstick baking paper
- 250g Stork (or butter if you prefer) plus a little extra for greasing
- 250g Caster Sugar
- 4 x Large eggs
- Zest and juice of 1 lemon
- 250g Self Raising Flour

The Prep

Preparing the Oven

Preheat the oven to Gas Mark 2 / Electric 150c / Fan 125c
Fill an oven proof dish with cold water and place it in the
bottom of the oven. This helps the cake stay moist and not
dry out.

Lining the baking tins

Start by preparing the baking tins. This is done first as once
the cake mixture is made it must go straight into the oven. If
the mixture is left out for any length of time the raising
agents will lose their effectiveness and the cake will sink.

To prepare the tins, start by tracing around both tins onto
baking paper using a pencil. Cut out the 2 circles.
Next grease the bottom and sides of both tins with butter
and put each baking paper circle into the bottom of the tins.

The Mixing Method

Making the sponge mixture

To make the sponge you can use either a stand mixer, a hand mixer or beat by hand (although that will be quite tiring)

- Start by zesting and juicing the lemon

- In a large mixing bowl, add the butter and caster sugar and mix together until they are light and fluffy. In a mixer on medium speed this will take about 2 minutes, by hand could take up to 5 minutes.

- Scrape down the sides of the bowl and add the eggs. Mix together for about 1 minute on medium speed.

The Mixing Continued 

Making the sponge mixture cont.

- Again Scrape down the sides of the bowl and add the lemon zest and juice along with the self raising flour. Mix on the lowest setting (if using a mixer) until the flour is just incorporated. If you are doing this by hand, fold the flour into the mixture, again until it is just incorporated.

NOTE: WHEN MIXING IN THE FLOUR, DO NOT OVER MIX. STOP MIXING ONCE YOU CAN NO LONGER SEE ANY FLOUR. OVER MIXING WILL CAUSE THE CAKE TO BECOME DENSE AND IT WILL LOSE ITS LIGHT AND FLUFFY TEXTURE

The Baking

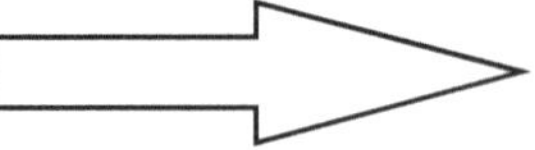

Baking the sponge

I bake my cakes on a low temperature for a longer amount of time. I find this ensures a nice light and fluffy sponge.

- Divide the mixture evenly between the 2 lined, greased baking tins.
- Place them on the middle shelf of the oven and bake for approx 45 mins.
- After 45 mins check the sponge with a cocktail stick. Poke the middle of the cake with the cocktail stick and if the stick comes out clean or with some light crumbs the cake is ready. If there is some cake mixture on the stick pop it back in the oven for another 5-10 mins, then check again.
- Remove the cakes from the oven and turn them out onto a wire rack to cool. If you find the sponge is sticking to the tin, run a knife around the inside edge of the cake tin to release the cake and try again.

The Buttercream
Ingredients

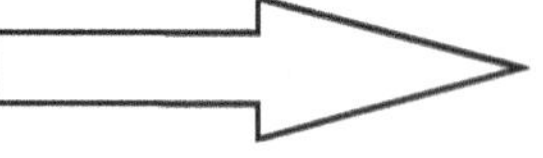

Buttercream

The buttercream i use in my cakes is the traditional
American Buttercream (ABC). I love the taste, and its so
simple to make.
This recipe will make enough buttercream to fill the cake
and possibly have some left to either cover the top of the
cake, or do a thin coat around the outside.

For the buttercream you will need:

- 200g Unsalted Butter
- 400g Icing Sugar
- Juice of 1 lemon
- Splash of cooled, boiled water

NOTE: I PREFER REAL BUTTER IN MY BUTTERCREAM BUT IT
IS A PERSONAL TASTE. IF YOU WOULD RATHER USE STORK
OR SIMILAR JUST SWAP IT LIKE FOR LIKE

The Buttercream Method

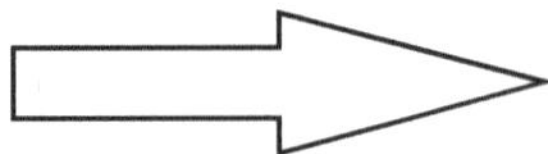

Making the buttercream

- Add the butter to a mixing bowl and beat on a medium setting untll its much paler and fluffy. With an electric mixer this will be approx 5 minutes.

- Add 1/4 of the icing sugar to the butter and mix together. Start on a low setting and increase to medium. Mix for approx 1 minute.

- Scrape down the sides of the bowl and add another 1/4 of the icing sugar and the lemon juice. Mix again on low before turning the mixer up to medium. Mix for approx 1 minute

The Buttercream
Method Continued

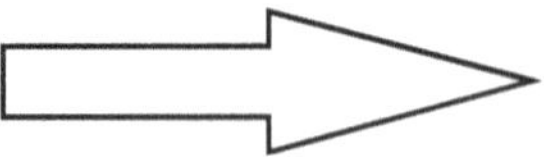

Making the buttercream cont.

- Scrape down the sides of the bowl and add another 1/4 of the icing sugar. Mix on slow before turning up the speed to medium. Mix for approx 1 minute.

- Scrape the bowl again and add the remaining icing sugar. Mix on low to start and turn the speed up to medium once everything is combined. Leave the mixer on for approx 5 minutes. This will make the buttercream super light and fluffy.

NOTE: IF THE BUTTERCREAM IS TOO STIFF ADD 1TSP OF WATER AND WIX WELL. ADD MORE WATER AS REQUIRED. IF THE BUTTERCREAM IS NOT THICK ENOUGH AND A SMALL AMOUNT OF ICING SUGAR AND MIX WELL. ADD MORE ICING SUGAR TO GET THE DESIRED CONSISTENCY

Assembling The Cake 

Assembling the Cake

Once the cakes have cooled its time to assemble them.

To Assemble the cake you will need:

- 6" thin cake card (or a serving plate)
- cake slicer/leveller (or bread knife)
- Small angled palette knife (if you don't have a palette knife you can always just use a butter knife)
- The buttercream
- A jar of raspberry conserve

The Stacking

- Start by levelling the cakes. To do this cut the top off each cake making sure to only take enough off the top to make it flat.

- Using a cake slicer or bread knife, slice each cake horizontally in half making 4 x thin (approx 1") layers.

Assembling The Cake
Continued

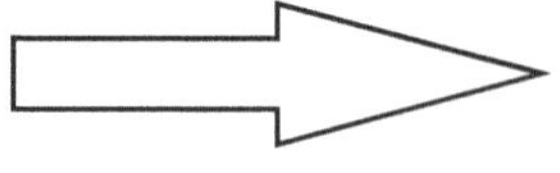

Assembling the Cake Cont.

- Place a layer of sponge onto the card/plate and spread enough raspberry conserve to lightly cover the sponge. Then add a thick layer of the buttercream on top of the conserve.

- Place the next layer of sponge on top and add another layer conserve and buttercream.

- Repeat this process until all layers are stacked. If you still have some buttercream left over, finish by topping the cake with buttercream or spread the buttercream all around the cake to make a semi naked design.

Troubleshooting

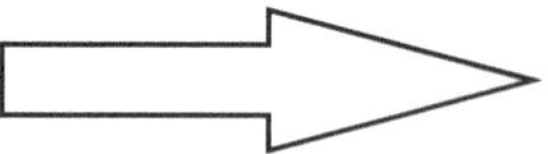

Troubleshooting

Sometimes things don't quite go to plan. Here you can find the more common problems and how to avoid them.

Sponge Mixture

Q. My mixture has curdled after adding the eggs?
A. That is perfectly normal and it will all come together when you add the flour.

Q. My cakes have sunk during/after baking?
A. There are a few reasons why this can happen:
1. You opened the oven door too early. This lets the heat escape and takes a while for it to reach the correct temp again. The cake looses its cooking momentum and deflates.
2. Its not cooked enough. If you take the cake out of the oven too early, before it is fully baked, the cake will sink in the middle.
3. Your didn't mix your eggs enough. Mixing the eggs thoroughly creates air bubbles which helps the cake rise whilst baking.
4. Your self raising flour was not fresh enough. If the flour has been sitting around in your cupboards for too long the raising agents stop working. Use freshly bought flour or flour which has only been opened recently.

Q. My cakes have a dome on top after baking?
A. The oven temperature was too high. When the temperature is too high it forces the batter up too quickly and creates a domed top. A lower temperature cooks the cake evenly, avoiding the domed effect.
Don't worry if you have a dome, just trim it off and you are good to go!

Troubleshooting
Continued

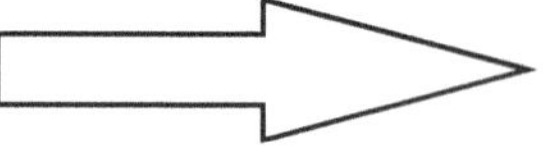

Troubleshooting

Buttercream

Q. My buttercream is really thick and stiff?
A. If you find the buttercream is too stiff, add 1 tsp of cooled boiled water and mix again. Keep adding small amounts of water until the desired consistency is achieved. It should be light and fluffy, almost mousse like.

Q. My buttercream is too runny/not thick enough?
A. If the buttercream is too runny, add more icing sugar and mix well until the right consistency is acheived.

Q. My butterceam is grainy?
A. A grainy buttercream means it has not been mixed thoroughly enough. Continue mixing the buttercream on a low / medium speed for a few more minutes.

Converting To Cupcakes

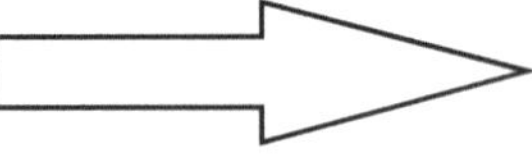

Converting the recipe for cupcakes
The Sponge

If you would prefer to make cupcakes, the recipe used for the cake will make enough mixture for 24 cupcakes. Just divide the mixture between 24 cupcake cases.

Oven Temp: Gas Mark 4 / Electric 180c / Fan 150c

Cooking time: 20 minutes approx. - After 20 mins lightly press the top of one of the cupcakes, if it bounces back after you touch it then it is ready. If a dent is left by your finger pop it back in the oven for a few more minutes before checking again.

If you need less than 24 cupcakes simply half the recipe for 12 cupcakes or quarter the recipe for 6 cupcakes.

Converting To Cupcakes Continued

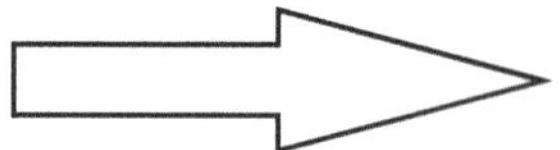

Converting the recipe for cupcakes
The Buttercream

If you are making 24 cupcakes, use the same quantities of buttercream ingredients as the cake recipe.
For 12 cupcakes simply halve the buttercream recipe, and for 6 cupcakes, quarter the recipe.
Using an apple corer or small knife, cut a small hole in the top of each cupcake and add a small amount of raspberry conserve into the hole. Approx 1tsp.
Using an open or closed star nozzle and piping bag, pipe swirls of buttercream onto each cupcake. You can finish each cupcake off with a sprinkling of grated lemon rind or colourful sprinkles depending on the look required.

Thank you!

Thank you for purchasing this recipe. I hope you like your freshly baked cake.

More recipes available include:

Chocolate
Coconut Cream
Chocolate Hazlenut
Red Velvet
Caramel Cappuccino
Salted Caramel
Cookies & Cream

This recipe is created and developed by me, Savanna Timofei. It has taken a long process of trial and error to get it right, and i am finally happy with the results. If you are happy with the results too please spread the word and get your friends to buy the recipe too. Please do not distribute this recipe. The recipe is protected by copyright and any distribution without prior consent is illegal.